Dear Parent:
Your child's love of reading starts here!

Every child learns to read in a different way and at his or her own speed. Some go back and forth between reading levels and read favorite books again and again. Others read through each level in order. You can help your young reader improve and become more confident by encouraging his or her own interests and abilities. From books your child reads with you to the first books he or she reads alone, there are I Can Read Books for every stage of reading:

SHARED READING
Basic language, word repetition, and whimsical illustrations, ideal for sharing with your emergent reader

BEGINNING READING
Short sentences, familiar words, and simple concepts for children eager to read on their own

READING WITH HELP
Engaging stories, longer sentences, and language play for developing readers

READING ALONE
Complex plots, challenging vocabulary, and high-interest topics for the independent reader

I Can Read Books have introduced children to the joy of reading since 1957. Featuring award-winning authors and illustrators and a fabulous cast of beloved characters, I Can Read Books set the standard for beginning readers.

A lifetime of discovery begins with the magical words **"I Can Read!"**

Visit www.icanread.com for information on enriching your child's reading experience.

For Timothy Driscoll
—L.D.

To the farmers who love their land and its inhabitants, quietly working away no matter the weather, seeking to leave a better land than they themselves received
—C.E.

HarperCollins Children's Books, a division of HarperCollins Publishers,
195 Broadway, New York, NY 10007

HarperCollins Publishers, Macken House, 39/40 Mayor Street Upper, Dublin 1, D01 C9W8, Ireland

I Want to Be a Farmer

harpercollins.com

Library of Congress Control Number: 2025939397
ISBN 978-0-06-327654-3 (trade bdg.) — ISBN 978-0-06-327653-6 (pbk.)

Book design by Jon Corby

26 27 28 29 30 PCA 10 9 8 7 6 5 4 3 2 1 First Edition

BEGINNING 1 READING I Can Read!

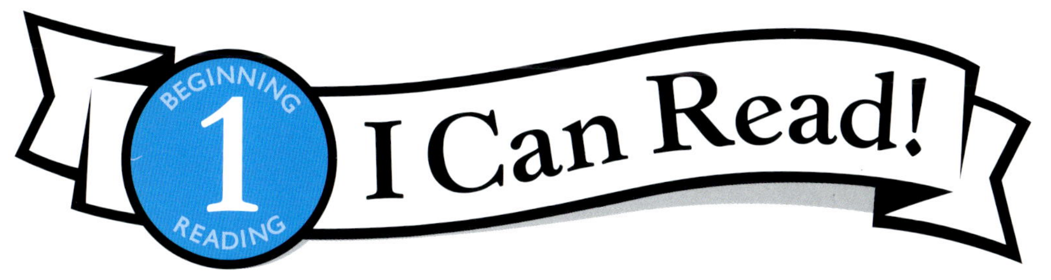

I Want to Be a Farmer

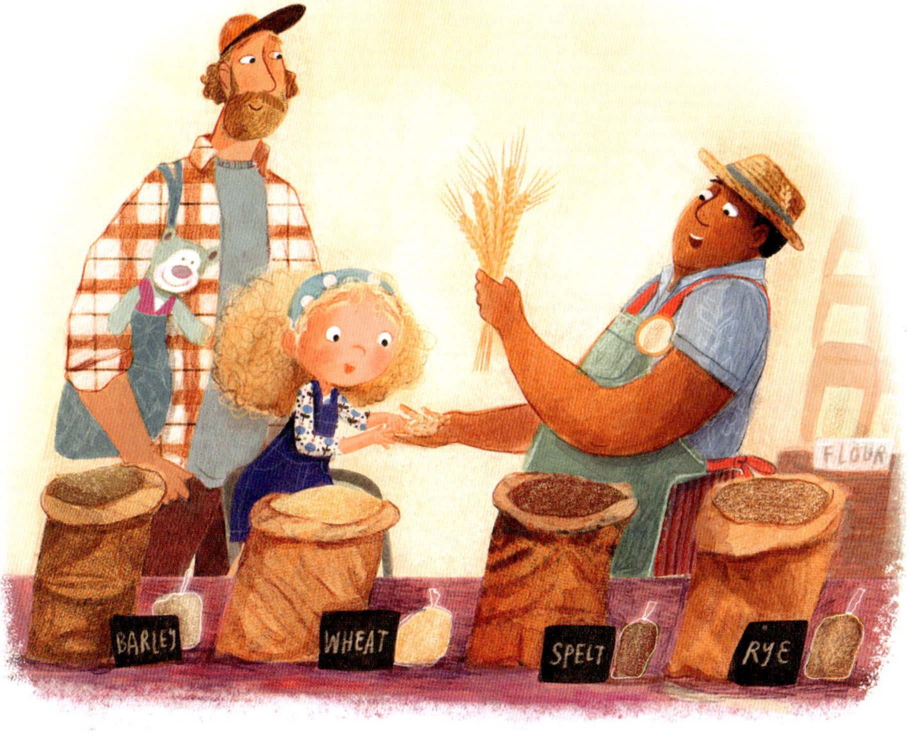
FLOUR
BARLEY
WHEAT
SPELT
RYE

by Laura Driscoll
pictures by Catalina Echeverri

HARPER
An Imprint of HarperCollins*Publishers*

My dad and I are at the state fair.

We can see it all from up here!

We eat cider donuts.

We play games.

And we bring my tomato
to the fruit and vegetable tent.
I grew it myself!
I enter it in the tomato contest.

Dad sees some farmer friends.

Cole is a grain farmer.

"I grow wheat," says Cole.

"It is ground into bread flour."

Matt is a vegetable farmer.

"I grow greens in water, not soil,"

Matt says.

Kim grows fruit.

"Our orchard has a brand-new kind of apple," Kim says.

I take a bite.

It is supersweet!

Other farmers raise animals.
Jane raises cows and pigs.
I learn that they graze
on grass on her huge farm.

“I call myself a rancher instead of a farmer,” Jane says.

Ted is a dairy farmer.
He shows me how
to milk a cow.

Ted’s farm has goats too!
“We use goat milk
to make soap and cheese,” he says.

The bird barn is loud with clucking!

Some chicken farmers

raise birds for their meat.

Maria raises chickens for eggs.

"Different chickens lay eggs of different colors," Maria says.

In the next barn, we watch
a sheep farmer shear a sheep.

A llama farmer invites us
to watch a fashion show.
All the clothes are made
from llama wool!

In another tent,

Nick is talking about honeybees.

He is a beekeeper.

"I take care of the bees,"

says Nick.

"And the bees make the honey."

There are even fish farmers at the fair!

Rita raises catfish in ponds.

“Raising sea life is called aquaculture,”

Rita says.

We meet so many farmers at the fair!

We meet a tree farmer

who grows Christmas trees.

We meet flower farmers.
They helped make
this sunflower maze.

We meet an herb farmer
in the rooftop garden.

“The sun helps the plants grow,”
the farmer says.
“And the garden keeps
the barn cool.”

At the end of the day, we head back to the fruit and vegetable tent.

But I can't find my tomato.

I look and look, and then I see it.

1st

My tomato won a blue ribbon!

I am a farmer.

And a good one too!

Meet the Farmers

Grain farmer
A person who grows plants—like wheat, corn, rice, and oats—that have kernels or seeds that can be eaten or ground into flour

Vegetable farmer
Someone who grows vegetable plants as food for people or animals

Fruit grower
A farmer who cares for trees, shrubs, or vines that make fruit

Rancher
A person who raises herds of animals on a large farm

Dairy farmer
A farmer who raises animals, like cows, goats, or sheep, for their milk

Chicken farmer
A person who raises chickens for their eggs, meat, or feathers

Sheep farmer
Someone who raises sheep for their milk, meat, or wool, which can be sheared off at least once a year

Llama farmer
A farmer who raises llamas for their wool, for carrying heaving loads, or for protecting other livestock from predators

Beekeeper
Someone who cares for one or more hives of bees that make honey

Fish farmer
A person who raises fish for food in ponds or underwater pens

Tree farmer
Someone who grows trees to be used as Christmas trees or to make wood or paper products

Flower farmer
A farmer who grows flowering plants for gardens or florists

Herb farmer
Someone who grows herbs to plant in home gardens or to sell at the market